GO VIRAL
GENERATING TONS OF TRAFFIC TO YOUR WEBSITE

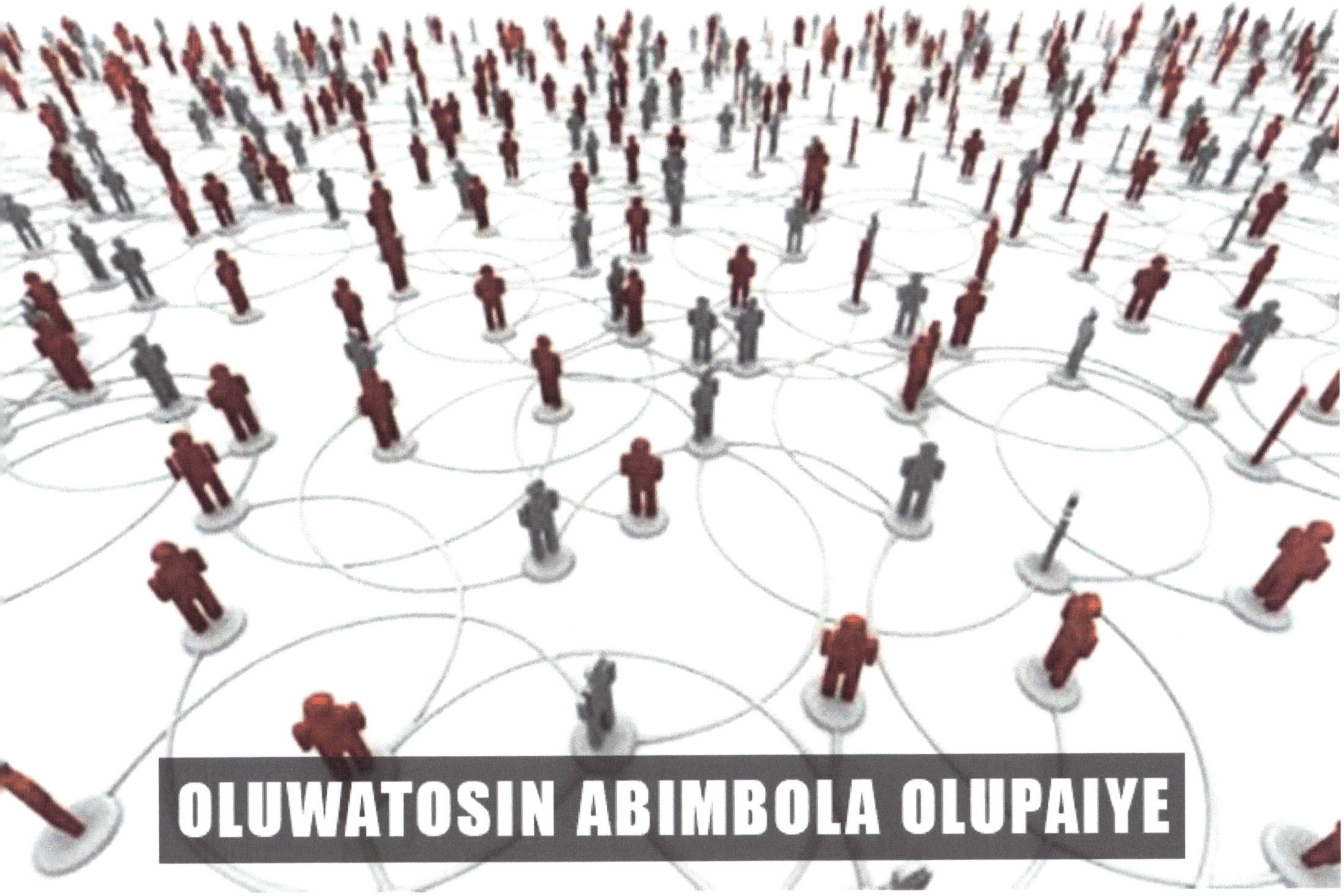

OLUWATOSIN ABIMBOLA OLUPAIYE

DEDICATION

This book is dedicated to God Almighty, my Everything. My best friend and lover Abimbola Joseph Olupaiye, my son Enoch Abimbola, my parents Engr. & Mrs Bola Adeyemi. My siblings Segun, Doyin and Bolade, my Inlaws, my friends and fans. I love you all!

Disclaimer

Please note that this eBook may be distributed freely or may be sold for a small fee as long as the contents within is not changed or ownership is overwritten. We advise you to print this eBook out in its entirety to help you get the most from this information!

This digital eBook is for informational purposes only. While every attempt has been made to verify the information provided in this report, neither the author, publisher nor the marketer assume any responsibility for errors or omissions. Any slights of people or organizations are unintentional and the development of this eBook is bona fide. The producer and marketer have no intention whatsoever to convey any idea affecting the reputation of any person or business enterprise. The trademarks, screen-shots, website links, products and services mentioned in this eBook are copyrighted by their respective owners. This eBook has been distributed with the understanding that we are not engaged in rendering technical, legal, medical, accounting or other professional advice. We do not give any kind of guarantee about the accuracy of information provided. In no event will the author and/or marketer be liable for any direct, indirect, incidental, consequential or other loss or damage arising out of the use of the information in this document by any person, regardless of whether or not informed of the possibility of damages in advance. Thank you for your attention to this message.

Contents

What Is Viral Traffic Generation? 5

Why Should I Use Viral Traffic Generation? 8

How Much Does Viral Traffic Generation Cost? 11

How Can I Make My Message Go Viral? 12

21 Viral Traffic Generation Techniques 14

1. Provide Quality Content, Products, Or Services 16
2. Give Something Away 17
3. Require A Referral 19
4. Create A Viral Video Clip 20
5. Create a Brandable E-Book 22
6. Blog 24
7. Use Social Bookmark Sites 26
8. Use an RSS feed 27
9. Provide Free Content For Other Blogs/Websites 28
10. Linkbait 29
11. Run Contests 32
12. Make it easy for visitors to refer others 34
13. Make It Easy For Readers To Email The Page To A Friend 35
14. Offer A Digital Game Or Tool That Carries Your Message 36
15. Offer An E-Comment Or E-Card Service 38
16. Build A Community 41
17. Write Articles For Ezines And Article Publishers 43
18. Employee evangelism 45
19. Set Up An Affiliate Program To Let Other People Market Your Product Or Service. 46
20. Write Press Releases 48

21. Take Your Marketing Offline 49
Conclusion.. 51
Useful Resources You *Really* Should Check Out! 53

What Is Viral Traffic Generation?

In recent years there has been more and more written about Viral Marketing and why you should be using it to drive traffic to your site. So, what is viral marketing, and why should you care? Is this just another fad that will soon fade away?

In short, viral marketing involves getting other people to willingly spread your message for you. People who like what you have done tell other people, and the message spreads from person to person like a virus. When that happens, it is referred to as your message "going viral."

It relies heavily on word of mouth advertising; someone sees or reads what you have to offer and tells a couple of their friends. Their friends see or read your message and they tell a couple of their friends, and they tell a couple of their friends, and so on. The number of people who are aware of you and your message increases exponentially. The more people hear about your site, the faster your traffic grows. How large will it grow? There is really no way to tell. The only real limit to the amount of traffic possible is how many people your site host can handle.

Just think about how quickly it could spread. If one person saw your message and told 2 people, who told 2 people, who told 2 people, and it continued, your message would very quickly be in front of thousands of people. If each person just told two other people, look how quickly it can grow.

$$1 \times 2 = 2$$
$$2 \times 2 = 4$$
$$4 \times 2 = 8$$
$$8 \times 2 = 16$$
$$16 \times 2 = 32$$
$$32 \times 2 = 64$$
$$64 \times 2 = 128$$
$$128 \times 2 = 256$$
$$256 \times 2 = 512$$
$$512 \times 2 = 1024$$

Now just imagine if you started with 100 people spreading your message, or 1,000 people. You can see that it doesn"t take long before hundreds of thousands, or even millions of people are aware of who you are, and better still, are visiting your web site and buying your products or services.

Viral marketing effectively taps into pre-existing social networks that your customers are already using. By creating something that is worth talking about and passing along, you create a "buzz" that spreads across the internet, and traffic floods to your site to see what the buzz is about. Once they are there, if they like what they see, they pass the information along, and the buzz continues to grow.

Word of mouth marketing is by far the most effective way to get word out about your site. People will listen to others that they already know and trust much more readily than they will listen to you. These people do not know you, so why should they trust what you are telling them? After all, you might be likely to say anything in order to make a sale. However, they will listen to a friend or family member, especially if the person spreading the word does not have anything to gain by telling them. It is just a friend passing along a great deal they found, or some useful or interesting information.

Why Should I Use Viral Traffic Generation?

You may be thinking that viral marketing techniques are only for the major players with big budgets, and that it can not work for small businesses with small budgets. If that is your thinking, I can assure you, you are wrong. You might not be able to afford to produce the highly polished ads like the big companies, but there are still a lot of opportunities for success. Any business or individual with a message to get out or a service or product to sell can benefit from a well crafted marketing campaign.

There are several reasons that you should be using viral traffic generation techniques to build your business and attract customers to your website.

1.)   It is a fast, effective way to drive traffic to your site.

Like I mentioned above, once the word starts to spread, it can spread very quickly, and there is really no limit to how many people can hear your message. Because your message often comes to someone from a person they already know, it has more credibility than if the message showed up uninvited in an email from someone they do not know.

Once the message starts to spread it picks up size and speed as it goes, like a snowball rolling down a hill. You may start out thinking that your efforts were not very effective, then one morning you open your email to find it full of new orders. When it works, it can work very fast.

2.) It can be very inexpensive.

Once the word starts to spread, there is not much additional cost. The biggest cost you will face is paying for all the additional traffic to your site. All of the cost and effort of spreading the word about what you have to offer is taken care of by the people spreading the word. More than likely, the biggest expense will be the upfront set up or production costs. Depending on which technique you decide to use. After that initial expense, the cost remaining costs are nominal.

3.) It can help shield you from negative comments

One thing to remember is that a negative message can go viral, too. Unfortunately, you are not going to be able to please everyone. If you do enough business, eventually you are going to have someone who is unhappy with you and your business. It only takes one customer that is dissatisfied to put a shadow of doubt in your customer"s minds about whether they should do business with you or not. Once that doubt is there, it is hard to remove it. If people are not happy with the service they received, they are more likely to tell people about it than if they are happy customers.

As unhappy customers start spreading negative messages about you, the word will start to spread, and there is not much you can do to stop it. The more it spreads, the more untrustworthy your business appears. All you can do is have enough of a buffer in place that the negative messages do not overpower the positive messages.

If your message goes viral, not only will is send a flood of traffic to your site, but other sites will link to you, and your site will rank higher in the search engines. Your name will also appear on other high ranking sites. If a negative message does start to go around, it will have a much harder time getting out, because your positive message is already so highly ranked that the negative messages can not find their way to the top of the search engine listings.

4.)   It can find hidden customers.

Despite the time and money you spend trying to narrowly define your customers, figuring out who they are, and more importantly, where they are, there will always be people that you have missed. Once your message goes viral, there is no telling where it will end up, or who will see it. Because of the widespread coverage that can occur, people that you had not even considered to be your customers will get a chance to see your message. They will decide whether they are potential customers or not.

As word continues to spread about what you are offering, you do not have to worry about finding all the possible niches your customers might be hiding. You do not have to go find them, they will find you.

How Much Does Viral Traffic Generation Cost?

The cost of viral marketing really depends on the type of marketing campaign you decide to use. With the 21 Viral Traffic Generation Techniques listed below, there are many that are free, or very low cost. Some may cost a little more to produce and get started, while others could become quite expensive. How much you spend is entirely up to you and the how you want to use the different methods.

One of the greatest things about viral traffic generation is, once you get the initial message out, it really doesn"t cost you any more once it goes viral. Your customers bear all of the time and expense of spreading the word. All you have to do is be prepared to handle the traffic when it comes. Depending on your website hosting service, there may be some costs for additional bandwidth as more customers flood your site, but if your sales increase because of the traffic it is worth the additional cost.

How Can I Make My Message Go Viral?

This is an often asked question, and there has been a lot of time and money spent to find the answer. The truth is, there is no guaranteed way to make your message go viral. There are some things you can do to increase the chances that it will take off, but you can not "make" it happen.

Successful viral traffic generation is part skill, part creativity, part timing and circumstances, and part luck. You may try dozens of things with no real success, and then strike gold in a completely unexpected place.

There is a quote that says "Luck is what happens when preparation meets opportunity." If you continue to market your site, and continue to lay the groundwork for success, you greatly increase the odds that you will be "lucky". For some sites it takes a long time to become an overnight success.

By presenting your message in a useful, unique or entertaining way, it encourages people to spread the word. It requires creating a message with a wide appeal, and has a high potential of getting passed along.

Once it begins, there is no telling where it will go, how far it will spread, or who it will reach.

If you happen to be one of the fortunate ones who have several messages going viral, you could easily reach millions of people. It does not happen for everyone, but it could happen for you.

21 Viral Traffic Generation Techniques

Below are 21 techniques that you can use to bring traffic to your website. Whether there is a flood or a trickle really depends on your ability to give your visitors something they can use or enjoy. It is important to remember that your customers are not stupid. They will know whether what you are offering is something they want, or if it is a cheap advertising ploy. If it is, they will pass the word along. If it is not useful, they will leave your site and say nothing to others about you.

The key to all of these techniques is to give something that adds to the user"s experience. This can be by offering useful information, telling them about something new and exciting, or something that is entertaining or humorous, but the key is to make it the highest quality possible.

With so much information on the internet that is just a click away, what you are offering has to be unique. This can mean being completely new, or it could mean looking at something old from a different and unique point of view. If your message does not touch them in some way, your message will not go viral. You may still get some traffic out of it, but that traffic will come the old fashioned way, through hard work, search engine optimization, and daily on-going marketing efforts.

While for many people, going viral is a one-time accomplishment, others manage to see repeated success. When one of your messages goes viral, not only does it drive a flood of traffic to your site on a short term, but many of those people will become subscribers, which increases your daily traffic. If you can continue to write unique, compelling material, those people will be more than likely to return to your site, and to tell others. The more eyes that see you message, the better your chances of repeating your viral success.

Viral traffic generation should not be used as a stand alone technique. It needs to be a part of a larger marketing strategy. Many of the techniques by themselves may only send a small stream of traffic to your site. That is why you need to use more than one marketing method. One stream may not amount to much traffic, but several streams could be significant. As your message starts to go viral, these several streams could quickly become a flood.

Look though the list of items listed and think about which ones will work for you. Chances are, not all of them will work for everyone. Some of them will naturally go together, others will not.

The list is not meant to be a comprehensive list of everything possible. It is meant to be a tool; an example of things that have worked for others. As you read through the different techniques, keep thinking about your own business. It may help you to come up with other ideas on your own. Be creative. Modify some of the ideas listed and come up with something new that is unique to you and your business. The only limit to what is possible is your imagination.

1. Provide Quality Content, Products, Or Services

Providing quality content, products, or service is by far the best way to build your reputation, and build repeat traffic to your site. Research has shown that on average, when someone has a positive experience they will tell two other people about that experience. On the other hand, if they have had a bad experience, they will tell seven other people. That act of telling others is how the viral traffic generation techniques start. If your customers never tell anyone else about you and your site, you are back to doing all of the marketing on your own.

To build returning customers to your site, you need to establish a reputation as an expert in your field, very entertaining, or someone who has unique insights. That does not happen if all you are offering is cheap, recycled drivel that you found on someone else"s website. Make sure that what you offer is your own work, and something that is different from what can be found on every other website.

As your reputation as an expert increases, other websites and bloggers will start to pay attention to your website. They will begin to talk about what you are doing, and will even give links from their website to yours. Suddenly every one of their readers becomes a potential customer. The higher the quality of material you produce, the more often your site will be linked to. Each link to your site is an avenue for new visitors to your business.

If you do not think you have the ability to create something that will touch people like it needs to, you may have to spend the money and hire someone else to do it for you. Fortunately for you, there are a lot of service that will put you in touch with freelance writers, site designers, and program designers. If you have an idea about what you want, chances are there is someone available to do it for you. If you are willing to take a chance on a freelancer who has not yet established themselves, you can often find one that will work for a low wage in exchange for the experience the job will give them. Be careful though; often times you get what you pay for. Make sure the work you get is up to the standards necessary to appeal to your audience.

2. Give Something Away

One of the best early examples of building a business by giving something away is Hotmail. Hotmail gave away free email services and email addresses free to anyone who signed up for one, and a lot of people did (and still do). Today millions of users have Hotmail addresses.

What made hotmail successful was one of the early successes of viral traffic building on the internet. At the bottom of every email that was sent through one of the free Hotmail accounts was a message telling others how they could get a free Hotmail account. Every time a

Hotmail user sent a message, they were helping spread the name of Hotmail.

How did Hotmail make any money off of free accounts? They did it by offering premium services to their customers such as additional storage space, and the ability to send emails without any advertising attached.

Hotmail became successful enough that in 1997, less than 2 years after it was created, it boasted over 8 million users and was purchased by Microsoft. It is still one of the top web based email services in the world.

While you may not be able to achieve the same amount of buzz that Hotmail was able to generate, it does demonstrate the power of getting your message out be attaching it to something that people are willing to share with their friends, family, and co-workers.

Do not discount the fact that people love to get things for free. If it looks interesting, and it is free, people are more than happy to give it a try. While it is easy to get them to try your offer initially, it is a different challenge to get them to continue using it once the novelty has worn off.

Repeated use is critical for your success because multiple exposures will cement your companies name in your customer"s minds. People are more likely to buy something from a company they have heard of than from one they have not heard of. They might not even know how or why they know the name, but that sense of familiarity will make them more susceptible to your message.

What ever you are offering has to be functional, easy to use, and add value to the user. You customers have to feel that it is worth their time and effort to pass the information along. Then, and only then, will they be willing to tell their friends and family what they have found.

3. Require A Referral

An added twist to the idea of giving something away for free to your customers is to require them to refer someone to you in exchange for what you are giving away. Simply provide a space where they can enter the email address of one or more people that they have to fill out before receiving the item you are offering. This is especially effective when your free item is something the person can download instantly.

This technique not only puts your message in front of the eyes of potential customers, it also helps you build your own mailing list. You can send an email the people that were referred saying "Your friend (name) saw this, and would like to share it with you. By having the ability to use the friend"s name, it helps to establish your credibility. This will decrease the possibility of person receiving the invitation tagging your message as spam.

Like many of the techniques listed, this will only work if your visitor thinks what you are offering is of enough value to make it worth giving you information about a friend or family member. Friendships are built on trust, and most people will not be willing to risk that trust on a worthless gadget.

Do not expect in instant flood with this method. It usually starts as more of a trickle, but that trickle increases the longer it flows. Over time, the referrals will add up. If each person that takes advantage of your free offer refers two or more friends, it will not take long to have quite a list of potential customers, all at no additional cost.

I personally use a script called ViralFriendlyGenerator.com to set up this viral marketing „word of mouth" campaign. It has added 1000s of subscribers to my list within months and I"m receiving new sign-ups to this very day from something I did years ago.

4. Create A Viral Video Clip

Have you heard of YouTube? If you spend any time online, it is hard not to have heard of it. Millions of people every day view video clips that are stored in the YouTube library. YouTube and Google Videos take advantage of the fact that people are now spending more time in recreational internet surfing than in watching television. It is another example of not only how people want to be entertained, but also that people want choices. The public has gotten used to being able to choose the entertainment they want, and not be forced to take what is pushed at them.

If you are creative enough, or cutting edge, or wacky enough, you could quickly be the next hot video. The videos that have the most chance of going viral are ones that deal with current events, especially if you can beat the major news outlets, videos dealing with business issues, and humorous videos.

Steven Colbert was a great example of this when clips of his Comedy Central show, The Colbert Report, were released on YouTube. Despite the objections of the Comedy Central network, when the show was still new, Colbert allowed clips from his show to be posted on YouTube. Within a short period of time his clips went viral, and viewership of The Colbert Report soared.

If you decide this is a method you want to use, make sure you have a fresh idea, and not a rehash of something that has already made the rounds. You don"t need network quality equipment to produce a decent video. While you do want decent quality production, the biggest key is great content.

Make your video, and at the end of the clip place a 3 – 5 second promotional slide with the URL for your website so viewers can look for more useful information. Make sure the landing page you send them to matches the tone of the video. If the video you use is quirky and humorous, and the landing page is serious and all business, your visitors will only stay for a few seconds before leaving for more entertaining sites.

Once your video is produced, and looks the way you want it to, upload your video onto YouTube and Google Videos. These sites offer services that allow website owners and users of social network sites like MySpace to place video viewers on their site. If your video goes viral, not only will potential customers be able to see your video on the host site, but also on all of the personal sites that pick it up. The amount of traffic that could flood to your site is huge.

5. Create a Brandable E-Book

Have you noticed the number of sites that offer free e-books to subscribers? Give your email address, click the link and you have instant access to an eBook full of useful information. The reason so many sites use this method of advertising is because it works, and here is how you can make it work for you.

Write a short eBook on a topic that relates to your business. In that book you include a little information about your business, and at a couple of key places include a link that will drive traffic from the book to your website. Now post it on your website and let anyone interested download a free copy.

However, it does not stop there. Encourage anyone who likes your eBook to offer it as a free gift on their website as well. If the information is useful, and the book is well written, the number of websites that are offering your book will begin to grow, Soon 50 or 100, or even 1,000 other sites will be helping you spread the word about your business. A successful campaign with timely information could keep driving traffic to your site for months or years to come.

Be careful not to overdo the information about yourself, or include too many links back to your site. The more about yourself you include, the less likely others will be willing to give your book away for you.

Another advantage of having your eBook before thousands of people"s eyes is it establishes your credibility. People give more credence to a published "expert" than they do to someone who has not written a book, even if the book is very short. You begin to build name recognition, and when people see your name associated with something in the future, they will be more likely to check it out.

Internet marketer David Meerman Scott used this successfully when he released an eBook titled *The New Rules of PR*. He posted a link to the book on his blog, and sent link by email to friends and colleagues. Within 3 days his eBook had been downloaded over 1,000 times. At that point it caught the attention of a couple of internet marketing gurus who talked about it on their own blogs. In the 3 days following those blogs Scott"s eBook had been downloaded over 15,000 times.

To date, the eBook has been downloaded over 60,000 times, and it has resulted in a continuing flow of traffic, and several speaking arrangements. He is now considered an expert in the field of internet marketing, largely because of his eBook.

Do a search for eBook compilers to find a program to create your eBook, or find a program that will allow you to save a document as a PDF. Whichever program you decide to use, make sure it allows you to include active, clickable links. If the person reading the eBook has to copy and paste the link into a browser, many of them will not. Make it as easy as possible for them to get to your site.

Also, make sure the program you use will not let anyone change the information in your eBook. There are less than honest people who will remove references to you and the links to your site, and include their own information into your eBook. Many programs will allow you to safeguard your information, so take advantage of them. [PDFBrandable](#) is an good piece of software that allows you to create brandable eBooks.

6. Blog

Of all the techniques I have listed, blogging is the most work to keep up with. It is also probably the slowest growing method on the list. In order for one of your blog posts to go viral, people have to know your blog exists. With so many quality blogs already in existence, it may take some time to get your blog noticed. It requires persistence.

Before you decide to begin blogging, make sure you are interested enough in the topic to write about it on an almost daily basis. For a blog to be effective, you need to post at least 3 – 5 articles a week. While the posts do not need to be long, they should at least contain the elements that any technique needs to go viral; a unique point of view on a subject, informational, entertaining, and fresh.

Not only do you need to be consistent in posting new information, you also need to work at marketing your blog. There are several easy ways to start getting other people to pay attention to your blog. Start by finding other popular blogs that cover a similar subject as you cover. Leave insightful comments on their blog. When you leave a comment, you can include a link back to your own site. If some reads your comment and like what you have to say, they may head over to your site to see what else you have to offer. If the blog you leave a comment on is very popular, this could drive a fair amount of traffic to your site.

Another method of getting your blog notice is to write a post on your blog commenting on something you read on someone else"s blog. You add a link in your post pointing back to the blog you mentioned. In blog language this is referred to as a "trackback". When you put the URL of the other blog in the trackback section of your blogging program it sends a message to the blog you are linking to informing them that you mentioned them in your blog. They come and read what you said, and if they like it, they may write something on their blog about your post. Their viewers can also click the link, which will drive traffic to your blog.

It is very easy to get started blogging if that is an area you are interested in. There are several good online blog services that will allow you to set up a blog for free. Some of these services, like Blogger.com, even allow you to set up AdSense advertising on your blog, which will let you earn a little extra income with your blog. If you would rather have the blog located as part of your own website, programs like WordPress are very easy to set up and use. The best part is, it is free to use.

If you write good blog posts, and can effectively market your blog, your readership will grow. The more readers you have, the greater the chances of one of your posts going viral. The key to success is quality material that is fresh, and holds the readers attention. You can not get away with recycling what you read on someone else"s blog.

When visitors come to your blog, make sure you give them a compelling reason to go to the main part of your site to look around. If your blog becomes popular, this method could drive a flood of traffic to your site that will continue on an almost daily basis.

7. Use Social Bookmark Sites

Something that has really flourished in recent years is the popularity of social bookmark sites like Digg, Stumble Upon, and del.ico.us. These sites allow users to search, set bookmarks, organize, read, and rate anything on the internet. If something you have written is posted to one of these sites, other readers get a chance to vote on whether or not they like it. If someone thinks it is good, and worth sharing, they can vote for it. The more people vote for it, the higher up in the rankings it moves. The higher it goes, more people see it. The more people see it, the more opportunities there are for someone else to vote on it, which helps it to rank even higher.

The good part for you is, even if a reader doesn"t vote on your article, they still might go to your site to see if there is anything else there that they might like.

One important thing to note is, these social bookmark sites do not like you to vote for your own articles. In fact, if you do vote for your own, it could cause it to move lower in the rankings. You have to have something that other people find interesting enough that they feel compelled to vote for it.

These sites attract hundreds of thousands of visitors every day. If you are fortunate enough to have your message ranked toward the top on one or more of these sites for even one day, the flood of traffic to your site could be tremendous.

8. Use an RSS feed

Another way to build returning traffic to your site is to provide an RSS feed. In its current form, RSS stand for "Really Simple Syndication".

RSS allows someone to place a link on their homepage, website, or RSS reader that sends an update every time you update the information on your site.

This is especially popular with news sites and blogs. If you are posting to your blog every week day, your readers will get an update 5 times a week. That means 5 times a week they will be reminded of your name and your website. This can really work to your advantage because they are getting that reminder because they asked to be reminded, not because you are forcing yourself on them.

Every day they have a chance to read your message, and have the opportunity to visit the main part of your site. The more traffic that comes to your site on a regular basis, the more sales and advertising revenue you can generate.

Another way to use RSS feeds is to bring news or information about your niche that will add value to your site. By putting fresh, up to date information on your websites main page, you give visitors a reason to come back to your site on a continuing basis. If they are interested in your topic, the will return to your site to get updates.

Both uses of RSS are designed to keep your customers coming back. The more often they come back and get new, useful, or entertaining material, the more likely they are of spreading the word to their friends and family, and that is the first step of going viral.

9. Provide Free Content For Other Blogs/Websites

Another great way to spread the word about your business is to provide free content to other websites and blogs. Everyone wants fresh, well written content for their website. Fortunately for you, not everyone has the time or the ability to do it themselves. With the ever increasing number of websites and blogs on the internet, there is an ongoing demand for article writers and guest bloggers. That"s where you come in.

By providing free content for someone else to use, they get useful information on their website, you get your name out, and they pay the marketing costs. It is a win-win situation for everyone.

Look around for blogs that cover your area of expertise and offer your services to them. They may want you to show them a sample of your writing before they are willing to take you up on your offer. After all, they have their own reputation for quality to consider. If you have a specific article in mind, you could show them the first couple of paragraphs. If you are extending an open offer, write a sample article that shows what you are capable of doing. Just make sure your sample displays the kind of quality they will be looking for.

After you write your article, you can place a short "About the Author" paragraph at the end. Included in that paragraph is information about your business, and more importantly, a link back to your website. Not only do you get a surge in traffic that comes from their website, but the more different places your material appears, the better the chances that one of your pieces will get picked up by one of the social bookmark sites or another blogger and starts to go viral.

10. Linkbait

The term "Linkbaiting" meets with mixed reaction among internet marketers. It refers to the practice of "baiting" viewers into linking back to your site from there site. You write something on your site that catches the interest of other website owners and bloggers, and they trackback to your site with comments about what you wrote.

The reason that linkbaiting is sometimes looked down on is that some marketers use somewhat controversial methods to get those links. While most of the methods are very legitimate, there are some that many feel cross the line, and are not appropriate to use.

There are several ways to get other site owners to link back to your site, many of which I"ve already discussed. The first is to provide useful information that is new, or a unique view of existing information.

The second way is to offer fresh, hot information. This is especially good if you are credited with breaking a story. When it works, this can generate a lot of traffic very quickly. The downside is, news stories have a very short life. The viral effect from a hot news story could be over within a day or two.

The third way is to use humor. People love jokes, cute or funny stories, and things that make you go, "hmm…" Everyone likes to be entertained. The trick is to get your message across, while being entertaining at the same time.

The fourth way to get links is to offer free tools or games that people can use from your site. Banks and insurance companies take advantage of this when they offer financial and loan calculators on their websites. While you are using the calculators, you are also being shown a message about other products and services that are offered. Even if you are not actively looking at the information, it is still planted in your brain, and builds brand recognition for the company.

The final method is the more controversial one. It relies on the power of controversy to get links. The way it works is for the site owner or blogger to take a contrary position on a popular subject, or to attack a popular person. Other blogs start to comment on what you said, either because they can not believe you had the nerve to post it, or they are coming to the defense of the person who was attacked.

The reason this is seen as somewhat controversial is that often times it is less than honest. The person making the post may not really feel that way at all, they only take that position for the passion, and links, that taking a contrary position it evokes.

The danger of this last method is the damage it could do to your reputation. If you are seen as a trouble maker or rabble-rouser, many of your regular viewers may leave your site and begin frequenting other sites that are a little more in line with their way of thinking.

So why would site owners risk damaging their reputations for links? The first reason is the immediate flood of traffic it can send to their site. Even though they may not agree with your opinion, some people will still check your site out to see if there is anything else controversial.

The second reason is that links represent popularity, and some search engines, most notably Google, use the number of sites that link to your site when they determine the ranking of each site. When other sites link to your site, it improves your ranking with Google. This is especially true with sites that are ranked higher than yours are. The more sites that link to you, the higher your site climbs.

For some site owners, the traffic generated by getting links outweighs the negative consequences that might come from a bruised reputation. For your business, you need to consider whether it is more important for you to have a quick burst of traffic to your site, or whether you would rather build a steady stream of regular customers that will continue to return to your site long into the future.

There are a number of sites that have effectively used gotten other sites to give them a link. Most notably are The Million Dollar Home Page, One Red Paper Clip, and All My Life For Sale. All three of these sites used unique ideas that made other site owners and bloggers want to write about what they were doing. The resulting surge of traffic made all three of these efforts overwhelmingly successful (and yes, the Million Dollar Home Page really did earn a million dollars).

11. Run Contests

People love to win things, and they love to be recognized for winning. Be creative in deciding what the prize should be, but consider how much your customers will think it is worth.

While prize doesn"t have to be something of great value, it does have to be something that is useful or of some value to the winner. Make sure that it is something they want, not just a blatant advertisement for your business. A bumper sticker marketing your web address is not going to generate a great deal of interest. Your advertisement or web address should be plainly visible, but it should not be the focal point of the item you are giving away.

If you are running a business to business website, free advertising on your site for the winner is something that wouldn"t cost you anything, but if your site doesn"t attract very much traffic the prize may not be seen as being very valuable.

The great thing for you is that running contests is a great way to drive large amounts of traffic to your site. Other than the cost of the prize, there is not very much cost involved in this technique. There are websites and blogs that are in the business of telling others about contests that other people are running. They will do your marketing for you. All you have to do is contact these sites and let them know about your contest. If it"s worth mentioning they will tell their subscribers. If the contest is good enough or creative enough, it may catch the attention of a blogger who will spread the word to others. The better the prize package, the faster and farther it will spread.

A good way to take advantage of this technique is to have a repeating contest, or a series of contests. This method will keep customers returning to your site. Not only will they return to sign up for the new contest, but they will also check back periodically to see what the next contest is, and when it begins.

12. Make it easy for visitors to refer others

Have you noticed the number of websites that include a button that lets you tell others about the site you are visiting? They are becoming more popular, because site owners have learned that if you want your visitors to do something for you, you have to make it as easy as possible. If you want viewers if your site to tell others, it does not get much simpler than giving them a button to click.

The nice thing is, if you design and set up your own site, it is quick and easy to add the button. The hardest part is deciding where you want the button located. If you do not do any site design, it is a small cost to have a designer do it for you.

The button runs a small bit of code called a "tell-a-friend" script. When your viewer clicks the button it opens up a small window that allows them to enter their friends email address and a short message so they can tell others about your site.

The power of this script goes back to what I discussed back at the beginning of this book; people will listen to what their friends and family say. There is a level of trust there that you can not come close to, at least not initially. That kind of trust is built over time.

13. Make It Easy For Readers To Email The Page To A Friend

Allowing your readers to send a link to your site through email is another way to encourage your visitors to tell their friends and family about your site. It is very similar to the tell-a-friend button in the way it works.

If someone likes your site, they have an option to click on a button that will open a window in their email program. The script the button activates will insert your web address in the message window of the email. They can then fill out the rest of the message and send your link to as many friends and family members as they like.

One reason this works so well is that the message come from someone they already know and trust, not from you. The email will not get stopped by the recipients spam filter, and there is a very good chance they will open it and read what it says

Like the previous method, it may not send a flood of traffic your way, but the traffic that does come is there because someone they trusted told them to check it out. They come to your site in a much more receptive state of mind, and more open to considering your message. They are there for a purpose, not just someone who is wandering through.

14. Offer A Digital Game Or Tool That Carries Your Message

Games are another thing that is very popular on the internet. I"m not talking about intensive multi-player games that take place in a virtual world, just simple games that people can play at their desk on a break at work.

If you or someone you know has any experience using Macromedia"s Flash, this can be an excellent way to get your businesses name in front of a lot of eyes. Like everything else, if you do not know how to do it yourself, all you have to do is look around and you will find someone who is willing to do it for you.

This is another area where being creative will serve you well. The game doe not have to be an entirely new idea, but the more unique it is, the more interest, and traffic, it will generate. Do a search for "flash games" and you will see thousands of games that people can play without any downloading or programs to install. You can also see that all of the games are not entirely unique. Some are simply a twist on an older classic game, but there has to be something different for it to work for you. The internet probably does not need another version of Tetris, but a Tetris like game with different shaped animals instead of blocks might get you some attention.

If your game catches on, there are quite a few sites that will advertise your game for you, and some that will even host a copy of your game on their site. When someone decides to play your game, you can put an advertisement about your business that they can see while they are waiting for the game to load.

One great example of using a free game for marketing is Peerflix. They created a game called "Paparazzi" that made fun of celebrities. The idea went viral and was quickly picked up by *Entertainment Weekly*, *E Online*, and most of the game sites. Within 90 days of the games launch, it had logged over 2 million unique visitors.

The great part for Peerflix is that nearly 5 percent of those visitors made their way over to the main part of the website, which was the reason they created the game in the first place.

Another option is to offer a free tool or resource that people will find useful. While some of these options might cost you a little more to develop and host, if they get exposure and become popular, they are an excellent way to get people visiting your site repeatedly. Calendars, organizers, and reminder services are all ways to get your businesses name in front of your potential customers. Quirky screensavers are another great program to offer. Every time the user"s computer sits idle for a few minutes, your message pops up on the screen. The trick is to put your message in a place where it can be seen, but it should not be the focal point. People are not interested in downloading your advertisement, but they will accept the advertisement as a small price to pay for something of greater value.

If your program works well and is seen as useful, users will tell other people about it, they will write about it on their blogs, and they will link to your program from their websites. That is what going viral is all about.

The great part about both of these options is it gives you repeated visibility. Marketing experts have determined that on average it takes being exposed to something at least 7 times before people will act on it. The more often people see your message, the more likely they are to do something about what they see. Advertisers and politicians put their message in as many places as possible so people will get exposed to it multiple times. That is what gets people attention.

15. Offer An E-Comment Or E-Card Service

Social networks have become an extremely popular way for people to stay in touch with each other. If you have not been to MySpace or Fac eBook, it is worth a look around. While a lot of the publicity these sites have gotten is because of the teens and college students that use them, businesses have discovered they are a useful way to build their networks as well.

Some of the sites are very bare-bones, but some of them are quite elaborate. One thing most of them have in common is a place for visitors to leave comments. Many times these comments are text messages back and forth between friends, but some of the messages are small digital pictures and graphics with a prewritten message.

There are web sites that provide these e-comments free to their viewers. If you see one you like and want to share with a friend, you can copy and paste a small line of code into your friends comment box, and the e-comment will appear.

When you look at these e-comments you will notice that on every one there is a company name or web address at the bottom. Most of these graphics are clickable links that will take the viewer back to the web site of the person that created it. If your e-comment is attractive or quirky enough, social network users will start sharing it with their friends. When their friends (or their friend"s visitors) see the graphic, they will click on it to see what other e-comments you have to offer.

While many businesses are using these services to build their networks, the majority of users are teens, young adults, and women. If your business is aimed toward adult men, this method may have limited success, but if you are marketing to the younger generation, you can bring a flood of traffic to your site with this method.

A similar service you can offer is free e-cards. People are always searching for cards to send to friends, family members, acquaintances, and co-workers. They are easy to use, and have maintained their popularity over the years. These cards come in several different varieties; with or without music and static or animated. Some are very simple animations; others are very elaborate Flash animations.

Once the person finds the card they like, they can fill in the message box, add the email of the person they are sending it to, and press the send button. An email is sent telling the recipient that their friend has sent them a card, and it gives them a link to click that will allow them to view the card.

The person receiving the card gets a message from a friend to enjoy and a small line telling them who sponsored the card. Because you are hosting the card service, the viewer is already at your site. You just have to give them a good reason to click the links that will take them where you want them to go.

In early 2006 job listing service CareerBuilder.com launched a program called Monk-e-mail. With the click of a mouse you could choose which chimpanzee you wanted to use with your card, then personalize that chimp with different clothing, glasses, hats, and backgrounds. Users also had the option of writing or recording their own message, and even had a text to speech functions that allowed the chimp to deliver your message. As an extra bonus, when you move your mouse around the screen, the chimp follows your movement.

Within 3 months of launching, over 14 million monk-e-mails had been sent. The kicker is that CareerBuilder spent no money in marketing this service. In the first week CareerBuilder sent out 1,500 monk-e-mails to employees and agencies, and word of mouth did the rest. Monk-e-mail was so original and quirky that the buzz quickly spread across the internet, and even maid it to the main stream media outlets.

You do not need to create a program as elaborate as monk-e-cards, but it does need to be creative and unique. If you do digital photography or graphic art, this could be a very good way to use your talent to build traffic to your site, or you could hire a freelance designer to create your cards for you. Do a search for e-cards and you will get a good idea of the types of designs people are using. As always, quality and uniqueness are an advantage.

16. Build A Community

One of the reasons for the ever increasing popularity of the internet is that it allows like-minded people to get together from anywhere in the world. From sports to politics to gum wrapper collectors; if it is something you are interested in, chances are very good that you can find someone who shares your interests.

Take a look at Yahoo Groups. They host hundreds of thousands of different groups from around the world. A search for "viral marketing" groups brought a list of 360 different groups.

While I"m not suggesting you try to become the next Yahoo Groups, it does demonstrate the desire for internet users to get together with people who share the same interests. One method you could consider to take advantage of this is to host a forum on your website. Find an area of interest that is related to your business, and set up a forum on that topic.

Allow your users a way to leave messages in the forum, or contact each other using email or an instant messaging program, and maybe even set up chat rooms where they can engage in active discussions. As the host of the forum you could help answer any questions, which will help to further establish you as an expert in your field. You would also help moderate discussions, and share new and interesting information.

Encourage your users to participate. Give them the ability to share ideas and to establish themselves as experts. Make it a safe, friendly environment where they can share their opinions (within reason). If your community stays active, it will continue to grow, and some of the community members will become customers.

You can find some very good forum programs that are available for free. Download the program and upload it to your web host and you are up and running. Many of the web host companies have software as part of their hosting packages geared toward building communities on your site. They make it very easy to set up forums, chat rooms, guest books and more.

Building a community in this way will bring people that are interested in your line of business to your website. Once they are there, it is easy for them to look around at what you have to offer them. Because they are already interested, it is much more likely that they will take advantage of what your business offers.

17. Write Articles For Ezines And Article Publishers

I mentioned earlier that people are more likely to listen to someone that they consider to be an expert. Why can"t that expert be you? If you know enough about a topic to build a business around it, you are an expert. All it takes is a little marketing to convince others that you are an expert.

One method of establishing yourself as an expert and gaining some exposure for yourself and your business is to write articles for ezines and article publishers. You write an article relating to your business, and then post it to one of the online publishing services. When people read your article, they see your name, and assume you know what you are talking about. The more different places you can get your name and the name of your business, the better that chances are that people will begin to remember you. Over time with multiple exposures you begin to build brand recognition.

There are two different ways online article publishers let you get your name out. Some sites, like ezinearticles.com, let you put a short 1-2 sentence "About the Author" section at the end of your article. You get the opportunity to put together a brief statement about yourself and your business, and a link back to your site.

Sites like Associated Content and Helium will have a content producer"s page that will allow you the room to write quite a bit more. You can talk about yourself, your business, and why the reader should believe what you say. You can also include multiple links that will lead the reader into your site.

When readers click on the link to come to your site they are what marketers refer to as "pre-qualified". They chose to be there based on the information they read. They were not tricked into visiting your site, and they were not pressured to go there by spam emails. They are there by choice, and that makes them more receptive to your message, and increases the probability that they will purchase your products or services.

Beside the traffic that comes to your site directly from your article, if the article is really good it may end up on one of the social bookmark sites like Digg, Stumble Upon, or del.ico.us. If your article gets ranked in one of these sites, it can bring a lot of visitors to your site in a very short period of time. That burst of visitors might last for only a day or two, but it could also linger in the top rankings for days or weeks.

Another side benefit of writing articles is that they can provide a small amount of residual income to you. Many of these sites offer revenue sharing that will give you a small portion of the advertising that the article generates. The amount you get per article usually is not very much, but enough articles over time can add up.

18. Employee evangelism

The best advocates you have for your business are already on your payroll. Your employees already have a vested interest in getting the word out about your company. If you succeed, they get to keep their jobs, but if you fail, they may find themselves unemployed.

Your employees know your business like no one else does. They can discuss the ins and outs of your business, and tell others why your product or service is superior to the competition.

Enthusiastic employees will spread the word to family, friends, and colleagues about your company, and you do not even have to pay them anything extra to do it. It is part of their normal conversation with people.

Back in the early days of the computer industry, IBM ruled the world of technology. A lot of computer companies were trying to get their legs under them, but IBM was the king. One of the reasons IBM was able to continually withstand the ever increasing competition was that they understood the power their employees had to market the company. They had a ready-made marketing team made up of engineers, secretaries, accountants, and programmers. By harnessing that power they were able to build a stellar reputation in the computer industry.

From the day they were first hired, IBM employees were taught how to be advocates for the company. They were trained in the company"s values, and were shown the quality of the products they were helping to build. They bought into IBM"s corporate culture, and they, in turn, shared what they knew with anyone who would listen. The technology world heard the message so often, and from so many different people, that they never questioned the fact that IBM was the best.

The key to success is your ability to assemble a loyal dedicated workforce. If you can do that, then you have the potential to tap into some of that power as well. Turn your employees into a marketing team and let them spread the word about how great your company is. If they truly believe it, their enthusiasm will become infectious. People will believe what your employees say, because it is obvious that your employees believe it themselves.

19. Set Up An Affiliate Program To Let Other People Market Your Product Or Service.

If you have never thought about using an affiliate program to sell your products, you might want to consider it. There are thousands of people on the internet that want to be able to tap into the online sales, but they do not have a product to sell. If you allow them to sell your product, you can have an unlimited amount of sales people marketing your product on a commission only basis.

The easiest way to set it up is to use one of the affiliate marketing sites like ClickBank or Commission Junction. There are several programs around, so you will have to do a little bit of research to find one that is appropriate for your product. For instance, ClickBank specializes in digital products. If you are selling an e-book or a downloadable software program, this might be the program to use. Commission Junction specializes more in tangible products.

For a small fee, usually a percentage of the sale, these programs will do all of the work for you. They will list the site in their searchable database where people interested in selling online can find you. If they are interested in what you are selling they sign up and become and affiliate sales person for you. They are assigned an affiliate code, and when someone goes to your site using a link containing their code, and makes a purchase, that affiliate gets the credit for the sale. The affiliate program tracks all of your sales, processes the transaction, and makes sure the correct sales person gets their commission.

There are pros and cons to using an affiliate program to sell your products. On the plus side, you have a motivated sales force that actively markets your product on the internet. They do the work, and take on all the expense of getting your message out to your customers. With a sales force of a hundred or even a thousand people, it does not take very long to reach a very wide range of potential customers. Even if people do not click the link to go to your site, it still helps increase your name recognition.

On the negative side, while it does not cost you much in terms of out of pocket expenses, there is significant cost involved. In order to convince someone to bear all of the expenses of marketing your product, there has to be ample compensation for them. Commission rates of 50 percent of the sale price are not uncommon for digital products. The rates for tangible items are lower, but they are still high enough to make it worth your affiliate marketers time and effort. The high commission rates will significantly lower the amount of profit you make on each sale. You can make up for this decreased profit with increased volume, but you have to keep a close eye on your costs to make sure you do not lose money on the transaction.

20. Write Press Releases

Like many websites, newspapers need content. A lot of newspapers, especially smaller local newspapers, have a hard time coming up with enough fresh content to fill all of the space they have. With limited budgets, they do not have the staff needed to come up with fresh material every day. This creates a great opportunity for you.

While papers are not just going to give you free advertising, they will allow you to write an article about something that your businesses is doing, especially if it involves a service or a community event. The newspapers understand that they are allowing you to advertise in exchange for the free content, but it cannot be blatant advertising.

All you have to do is write the article, making sure you mention your businesses name, and list your web address so they can get more information. You just have to make sure the piece is well written, and that your business is doing something worth telling people about.

Not only does this get the name of your business out to the community, but it also helps enhance your reputation. Even without knowing you, people will make a judgment on whether they like you, and can trust you. By building a positive reputation as someone who is active in the community, it makes it easier for them to like you, and by extension, your business.

21. Take Your Marketing Offline

Believe it or not, there are still people out there that do not get all of their information online. They use the internet for business or email, and occasionally will shop online, but if you want to reach them you will have to do it offline.

There are a lot of ways to make people aware of you offline. Some are better than others, depending on your business, but they all share a common purpose with the online techniques; get your businesses name front of as many people as you can, as often as you can. Sales people use the term, "It"s a numbers game." If more people get exposed to your message, more people will go to your site. More people at your site will mean more sales.

From pens to calendars to neckties, company names, logos, and web sites appear everywhere. Some companies have built a strong enough brand that people will pay to wear their logo. Coke and M&M"s are just two of many corporate brands that people proudly display.

There is a small sporting goods store I know of that prints and gives away hundreds of shirts every year. Anyone even remotely involve in local sports has at least one shirt form this store. At any casual event in town at least one person will show up with a shirt bearing that stores name and logo. I have seen pictures from as far away as the

Dominican Republic wearing one of those shirts. Anyone new in town or from any of the surrounding towns quickly learns where to go for their sporting goods.

A quick search online will give you a wide range of companies to chose from that specialize on providing promotional materials. There is a wide range of quality, price, and products to choose from, so depending on your budget, you should be able to find something that matches with what you want to accomplish.

Conclusion

The key is to get your name and your website address noticed as often as possible, and in as many different places as possible. Do not limit yourself to the items that were mentioned here. If you think it might be a good idea, try it and see. You might strike gold in areas where others have tried and only found limited success. It all depends on you, your product, and your ability to catch people"s attention.

Using viral traffic building techniques is a great way to bring a flood of traffic to your site. Some of the methods in this book will be a perfect for you and your business; others may only have a limited use, or not be useful at all. It all depends on what you want to do with your marketing. You have to decide which one will work best for you. The danger is to start trying to build a viral marketing campaign before your website is ready.

It is natural to be anxious about getting people to come to your website, after all that is the way online businesses make their money, but if you are not ready, you could lose a great opportunity. Many businesses try repeatedly to get their message to go viral with only limited success. Even those marketers who are very successful at it will tell you that it does not happen every time.

You need to be very clear about why you want people to come to your website, and what it is you want them to do once they get there. Are you selling a product or service? If so, make sure your sales letter is compelling enough to get the visitor to respond to your sales pitch and make a purchase. If you are relying on pay-per-click advertising, you need to make sure the content on your site is interesting enough that your visitors will return to see what other things of interest are on your site.

Take a good, objective look at your website. Once the traffic comes, what will they do when they get there? You have to make sure your design is right, your website is easy to navigate through, all of the links are working, and your message will convince people to do what you want them to do.

A final reminder; any one of these methods are not meant to be used as the only marketing you are doing. They should be used as a part of a larger marketing campaign. Everything you do to spread the word about your site can bring you traffic. Only a few of them will ever go viral, but each of them has the potential to send traffic to your site, even without going viral. Do not waste opportunities waiting for something to happen. Continue working on building traffic to your site, and being ready when the traffic arrives.

Be prepared. When one of your marketing techniques does go viral, hang on for a wild ride. It will all be worth your efforts.

www.ingramcontent.com/pod-product-compliance
Lightning Source LLC
Chambersburg PA
CBHW051055180526
45172CB00002B/650